# Jack's birthday

Story by Jenny Giles
Illustrations by Betty Greenhatch

"A car for me," said Jack.

"A red car!

Thank you, Mom and Dad."

"Look!" said Jack.

"My car can go

up and down."

"Here is a garage

for my red car,"

said Jack.

"My car can go

in the garage."

"Mom! Dad!" said Jack.

"Look!

My car is in the garage."

Jack said,

"My car is not in the garage!"

Dad said,

"I can see the red car."

"Look," said Dad.

"Here is Billy,

and here is the car."

"Jack's red car
is in the garage,"
said Billy.

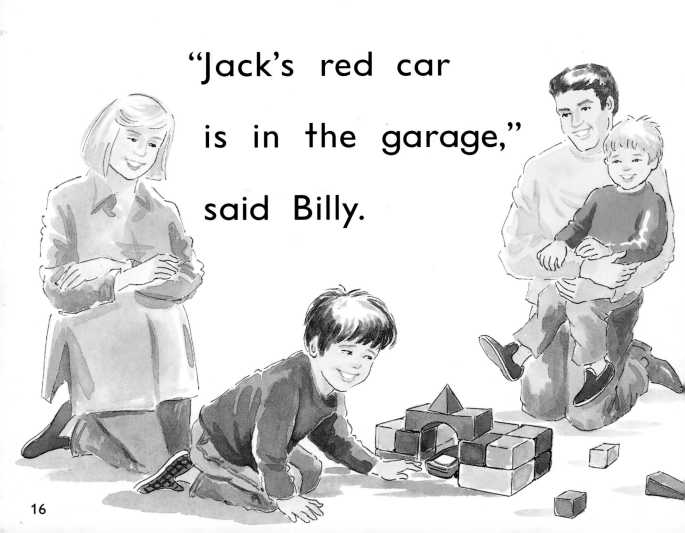